# Cover photo

Deb, Karen, Lynetty, Stephanie, Jan, and Carol

I'd like to personally thank the Pacemates used in the cover photo and all the Pacemates throughout the years who helped make taking Pacer publicity pictures glamorous.

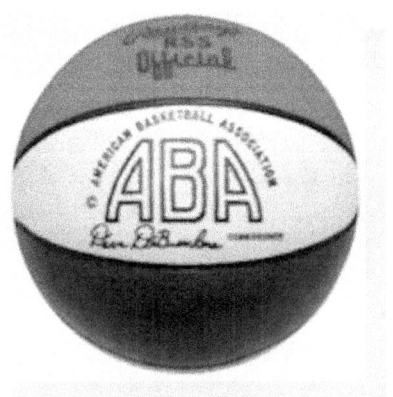

# ABA & NBA
# Through the Eye of a
# Photographer

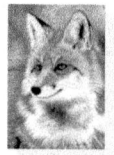

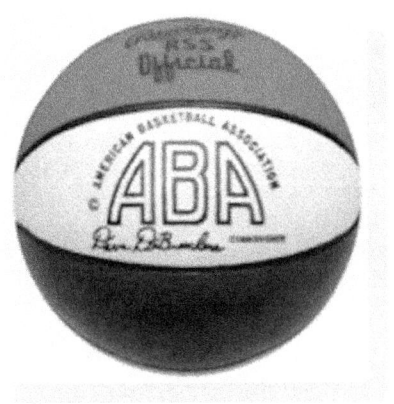

# ABA & NBA
# Through the Eye of a
# Photographer

## Steve Fox

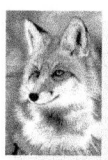

I dedicate this book to Dad, who loved the Indiana Pacers and the American Basketball Association as much as I did.

# Acknowledgments

**Larry Kaiser:** My teacher and good friend

**Arthur Hundausen:** This book would not have been possible had it not been for Arthur's foresight in collecting my ABA photographs of a bygone era. Arthur is the webmaster of "rememberingtheaba.com"

**Christina Guthrie:** Book editor, Guthrie Writing & Editorial, LLC, Indianapolis, IN

**Tim Fox:** Cover and back illustrator

**Robert Fox:** Offers of timely advice

**Nancy Zimmerman:** Timely words of encouragement

**John Ritchison:** Intellectual Property Law, Anderson, IN

# Table of Contents

# Introduction

I am writing this book now because it is something I had always wanted to do, and this was the right time in my life to share some of my experiences. I was fortunate to have been with the Indiana Pacers beginning in 1969 as a photographer, and at the age of seventy-four now I thought I would be ready for this new adventure by writing about my early years in the ABA and NBA.

The writing of this book was certainly a learning experience like no other. Learning Microsoft Word was a real challenge, but in the end, completing this book has been one of my most fulfilling accomplishments.

E-mail address
sfl11941@yahoo.com

# Chapter 1
# My Beginnings
# in the
# ABA

## My First Pacer Cover

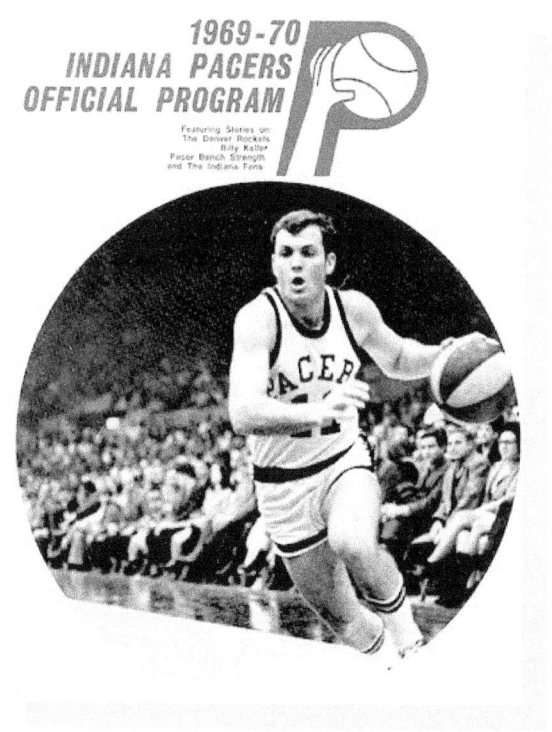

Billy Keller
Steve Fox photo

# My Early Games

I had never been to a professional basketball game before, but it would end up being the first of many.

My brother-in-law had business dealings with Bobby Leonard, and I asked him if he could get a photographer's pass for me, which he did.

As I entered the Fairgrounds for the first time, the building seemed old, even for the late sixties. I believe it held about 9,300 people, which I later realized was normal for a Pacer game, as most games were sold to capacity.

As the game went on during the night, cigarette smoke would fall below the lights, clouding out some of the light over the basketball floor that I would need to take pictures. This was long before nonsmoking laws were put into effect in Indiana.

I had photographed many high school games, but I was not prepared for how physical pro games were. Being only six feet away from the action, I got a close-up view of the arms, trunks, and anything that a defensive player could get a hold of to stop an offensive player's movement. I marveled at the sheer physical size of the centers and the forwards and the quickness of the guards. I took in the constant use of foul language, the squeaks, and rubber smell of basketball shoes sliding on the floor, the constant chatter of the referees to players during the game: "Keep your hands off him! Don't hold. Stop traveling, I'm going to call you on that! Stay out of the lane." Of course, all the warnings were ignored. The referees would blow their whistles, and the fouls were called—the players telling referees they were innocent of the foul even after being warned ten times, followed by the coaches disbelieved mode. A six-foot referee yelling at a seven-foot center or forward made the game interesting, and that's why people tried to get front-row seats at Pacer games because all the action was up so close.

# ABA Rookies

I still remember the rookies that came out of college and turned pro, thinking they could run the legs off the old pros. They would play maybe four minutes of the first quarter and have to be pulled out of the game, worn out, while the old pros would play ten minutes a quarter and then some. It would take several games to work the rookies into shape.

I do remember two exceptions: Michael Jordan and Julius Erving. They both came into the professional game as pros right off the bat.

One of the things I remember most is watching the development of rookies into pros. Not that they were not good coming out of college, but I enjoyed seeing them mature to men, and fine-tune their game.

# Bud Jones

Bud was the first Pacer team photographer, having started in the 1967-68 season, which was the beginning of the American Basketball Association.

Bud was small in stature with a white mustache, and he had an easy-going personality and would answer any question if asked.

I was a staff photographer for a couple years at the Indianapolis Motor Speedway, and I worked with Bud who was the chief photographer then.

I knew him as a very knowledgeable and capable photographer, so I knew at least one other photographer at my first Pacer game in 1969.

# The Red, White, and Blue Ball

The first thing I noticed as I walked out to the court was the red, white, and blue basketball.

I thought that ball had to be the best marketing tool one could ever imagine for a startup professional basketball league.

The photography back then was mainly black-and-white, and pictures with the ball in them really stood out. It was a photographer's dream come true. Color pictures were outstanding as well. It put a new dimension in sports photography.

If you were to buy one of those red, white, and blue basketballs in its original Rawlings box today, you could expect to pay $1,000 to $1,500.

Kids today still have them on the basketball courts around the country.

# The End Of My First Year in the ABA

This was my first pro experience, and it was everything I had hoped it would be—from the pregame preparation to the ball boys doing their jobs (I never realized how much they do before and after a game) to the Pacer Pacesetters exciting the crowd and helping give the fans an exciting evening. From my close-up photographer's view of the game, I was able to witness the physical endurance of the players, the quickness of the guards, and the intensity of Coach Bobby Leonard guiding his team. My first pro experience was more than I expected, and there would be many more to come.

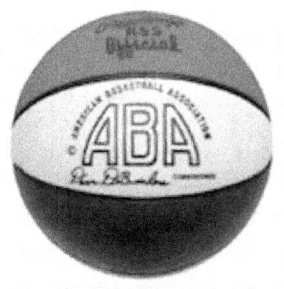

Roger Brown

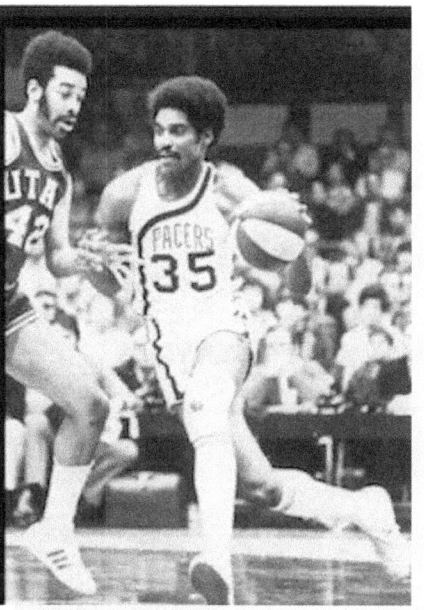

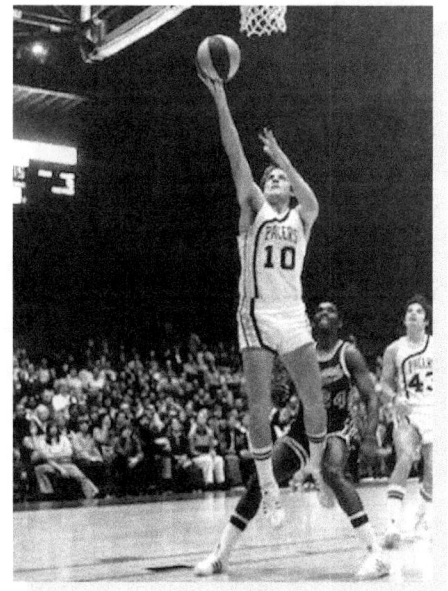

Don Buse

Steve Fox photos
Arthur Hundausen Collection

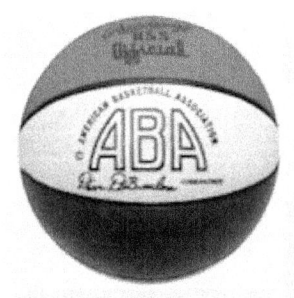

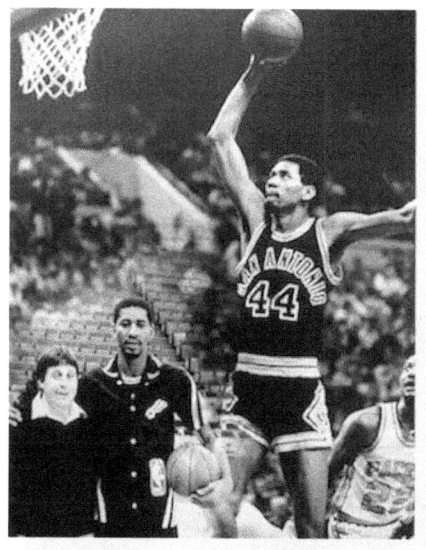

George Gervin

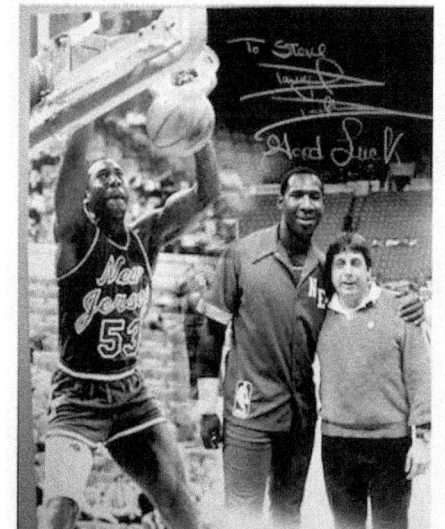

Darrell Dawkins

Martin Fox photos

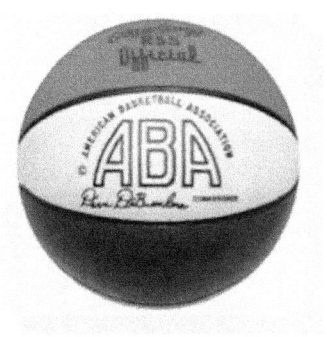

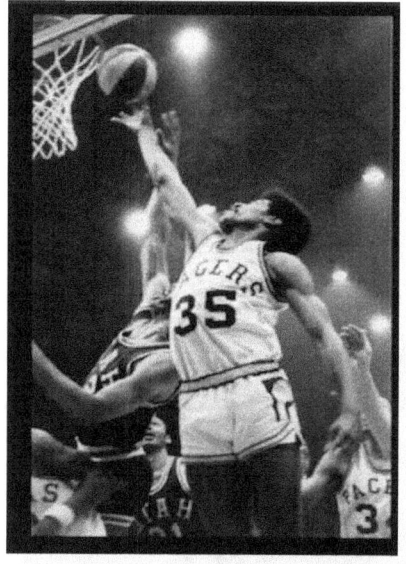

Roger Brown

George McGinnis

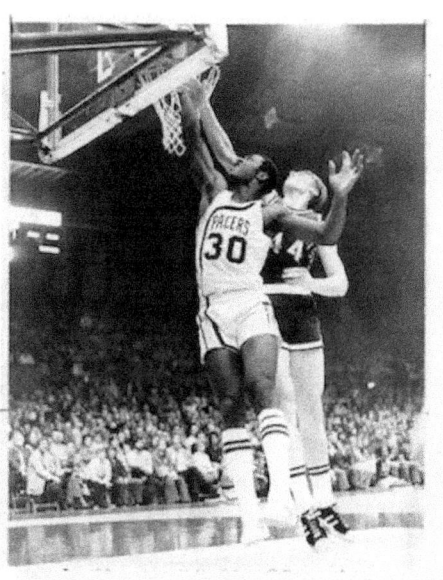

Steve Fox photos
Arthur Hundausen Collection

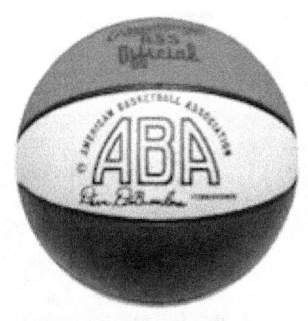

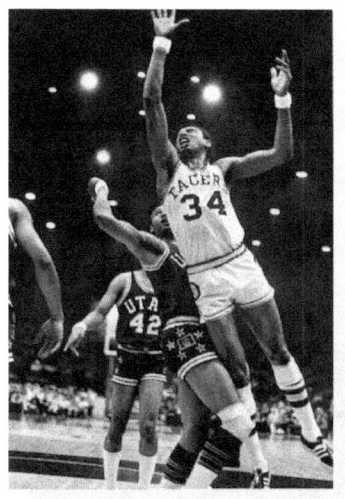

Mel Daniels

George McGinnis

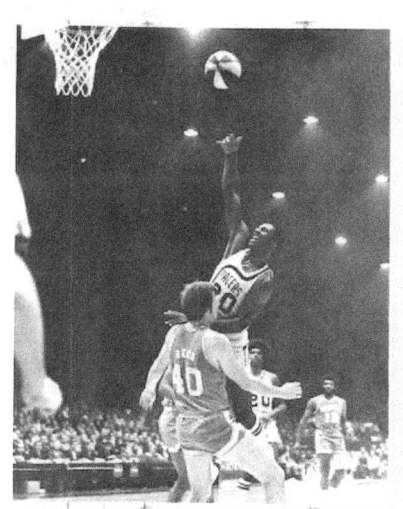

Steve Fox photos
Arthur Hundausen Collection

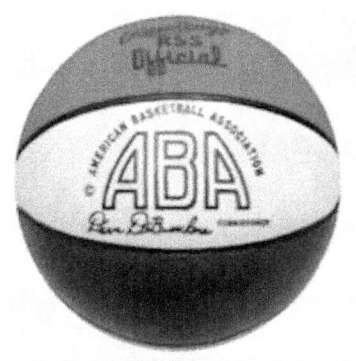

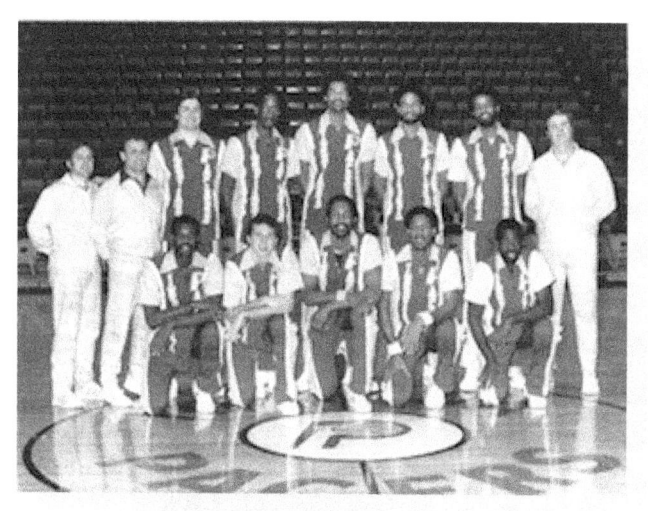

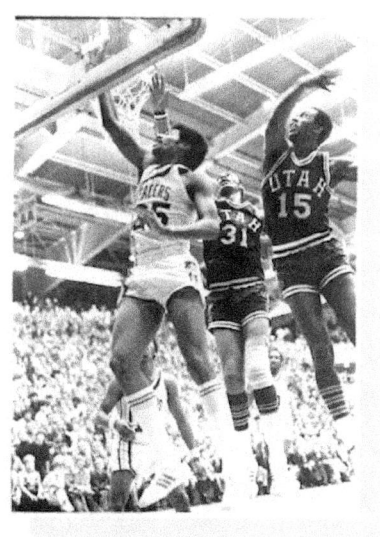

Roger Brown
Steve Fox photos
Arthur Hundausen Collection

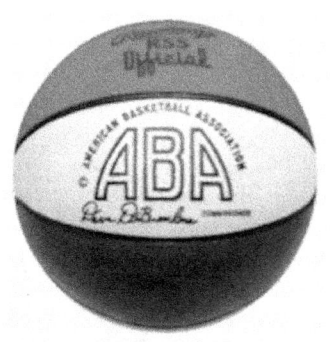

# Chapter 2

# My Years in the ABA

George McGinnis
Indiana State Fairgrounds Coliseum

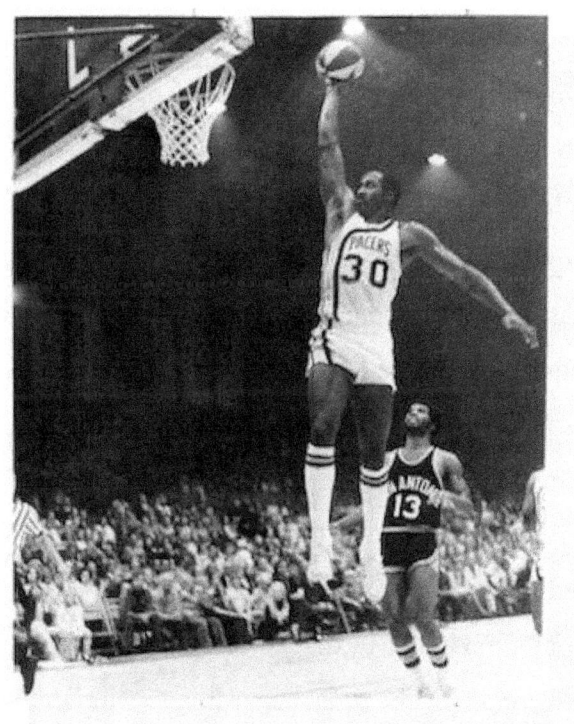

Steve Fox photo
Arthur Hundausen Collection

# Murderers' Row

Located at the east end of the Coliseum at floor level on the front row was "Murderers' Row," which was where Nancy Leonard and her friends were seated.

I still remember the actions of Murderers' Row. They were situated next to the visitors' bench and would collectively let the players and coaches have it, never relenting, waving their gold scarves. Sometimes I almost felt sorry for the coaches, knowing when they came to Indy to play the Pacers it would be a long three hours to play the game.

The referees didn't escape the wrath of the ladies either. They also knew that they too would be in for a long evening. During the game the referees would sometimes ask Murderers' Row if they made the right call, and half the time, according to Murderers' Row, it wasn't. It was always in good humor, and the fans would enjoy their antics.

I always thought Murderers' Row was the Pacers' secret weapon.

# Working with Nancy Leonard and Sandy Knapp

I worked directly for both Nancy Leonard and Sandy Knapp. Nancy was the assistant general manager of the Indiana Pacers, and Sandy was head of marketing. I remember Sandy working in the small Indiana Pacers office just east of the Coliseum, which at one time was a small business store. Sandy had the job of not only marketing but also organizing the Pacesetter girls for the pregame activities. Several of the Pacesetters (or Pacemates, as they were later named) worked in the same office with Sandy.

Nancy and Sandy would give me my evening photo assignments and the subject matter they wanted in the pictures, which we would go over before the game. I was always impressed with the knowledge they had and what they wanted the photos to contain. It really helped me organize my limited time before each game.

As I looked back at the years I spent working with
Nancy and Sandy, I can definitely say they were two of
the most qualified, organized people I know. What a
pleasure being around such nice people who treated me
like family.

My assignments besides the game action might be
setting up photo sessions with the governor, mayor,
business people, and other celebrities. Over the years I
have taken pictures of the Indianapolis 500 drivers,
Playboy centerfold girls, and of course they all were
looking to have their pictures taken with the players.
Those photo nights were always enjoyable and made
each game an interesting evening.

# Five-Day Road Trip

My first extended road trip with the Indiana Pacers was
in February 1974, and I was able to have my dad come
along. The Pacers were nice enough to give my dad a
photographer's pass for the season, and they had no
problem with him taking the trip with me. This was a
five-day road trip, playing two teams. The first game

was with the Carolina Cougars, which was sold out. From a photographer's point of view, sellouts are best because the seats in the background are full of people. Otherwise, the photos can look like scrimmage games with all the empty seats in the background. The next game would be with the Virginia Squires in Richmond, Virginia, and the last game was again with the Squires, but this time in Fort Wayne, Indiana. In each of those games we were lucky to have two or three hundred people in the stands. You knew early in the days of the ABA that some teams would survive, but others wouldn't.

The games were just a little part of the road trip. The fun really started while on the planes going to each game. I was able to see the players in a more personal way. To make time go faster while on the plane a poker game would start with more cash being wagered than I made in two months at my job with General Motors. The poker games didn't stop on the planes but continued at the hotel rooms late into the night. Coach Leonard and trainer Davey Craig stayed the floor above the team's rooms, hoping to get a night's sleep. No matter how late the players stayed up the night before, the guys were always ready to play the game the next night.

Some of the planes for the players in those days were certainly not fancy. Sometimes the team flew commercial, most always coach. Other times they a chartered a plane, and the pilot himself would load all the baggage, equipment, and personal luggage. Everything had to be weighed, and then the fuel was added. You just hoped that there was enough fuel to get you to the next city. This particular Piedmont Airliner was obviously under a lot of stress because of the heavy load. It barely cleared the security fences at the end of the runway. Is certainly was exciting to be part of this trip as a team photographer, but I was glad to make it home.

# ABA Friends

In my job as team photographer I was privileged to have met most of the players over the years in both the ABA and the NBA. I've always found the players to be not only great athletes but also good friends. I want to focus on some of the players I worked with not only as team photographer but also later in my work as a color oil artist.

1.  Mel Daniels

Mel passed away in November 2015 as I was writing this book. I was shocked and saddened by his passing. Mel could play offense and defense and was arguably the best center in the ABA at that time.

2. Billy Keller

 Billy did it all—jump shots, three-pointers, assists, you name it. And he could drive to the basket around those giant players with ease.

3. George McGinnis

George was always in action either on defense or offense. I was always guaranteed great action shots when he had the ball. He was one of the best players to photograph.

4. Don Buse

He had the quickest hands in basketball. You could always depend on him to lead the steels and assist on the court. He was also on the 1976 NBA All-Star team. A great guy to meet.

## 5. Darnell Hillman

Another guy with a great nickname, "Dr. Dunk" as he was called, won the 1976 NBA All-Star dunk contest. He was a great rebounder. I was never sure of his true height since he had one the largest Afro haircuts in pro basketball.

## 6. Freddy Lewis

He was a steady player who could play both ends of the court with ease. Freddy was another player who would get me great shots.

## 7. Roger Brown

Another great ABA player that passed away. There's nothing I can say that hasn't already been said about him. He had the ability to fake players out of position. The Pacers were very fortunate to have him on their team.

## 8. Bob Netolicky

Anybody who followed the early ABA days would know him as "Neto." He was one of the favorites Coach Leonard like to yell at. I can still see Neto looking at Mel Daniels as they were running down the court, mouthing, "What did I do wrong?" Fun aside, he was a great forward and a true friend of Mel Daniels.

I wouldn't know where to start naming the friends and other nice people I've met throughout the years during the life of the ABA. We were all in the same family. Now our days of the American Basketball Association are but a fond memory.

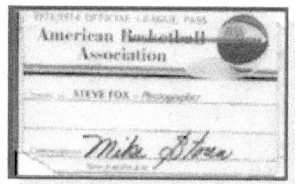

ABA league pass

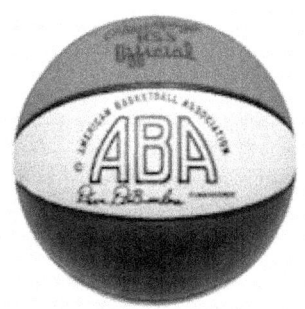

# Mel Daniels

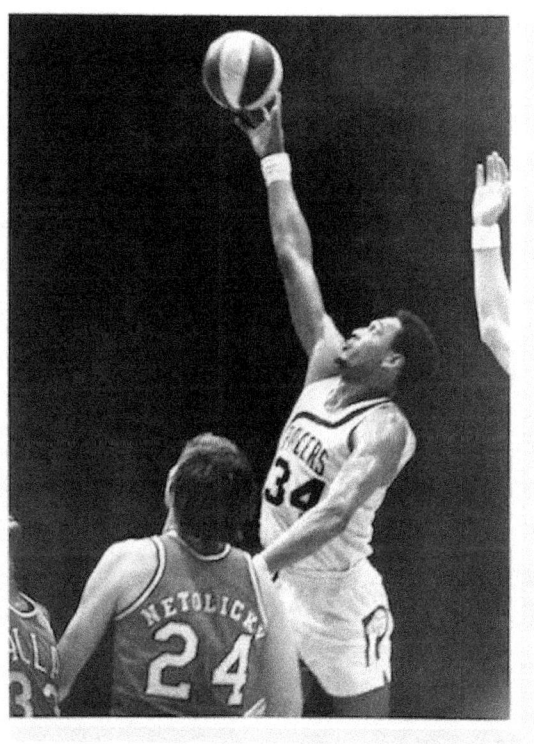

Steve Fox photo
Arthur Hundausen Collection

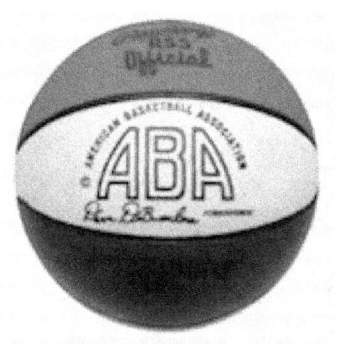

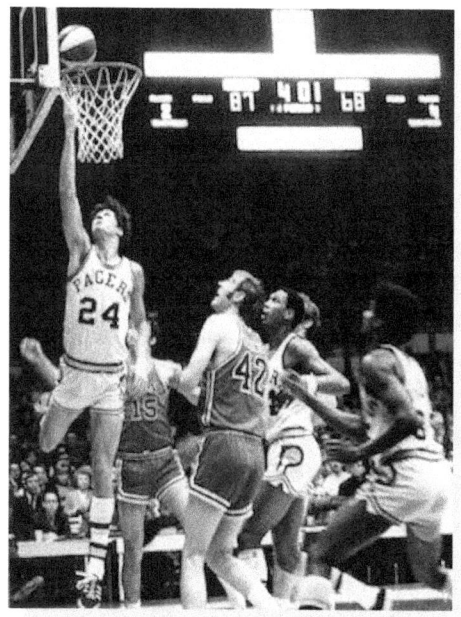

Bob Netolicky

Freddie Lewis

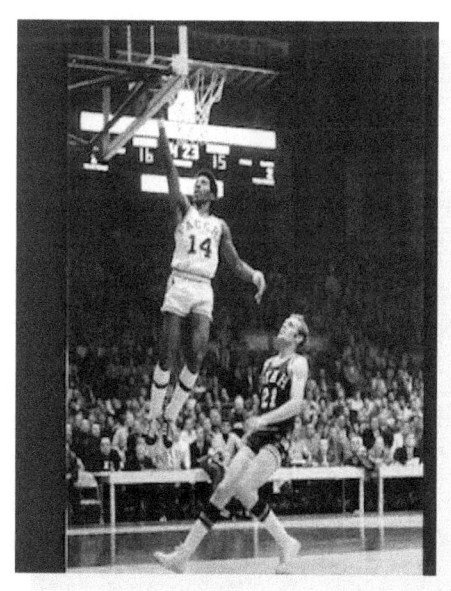

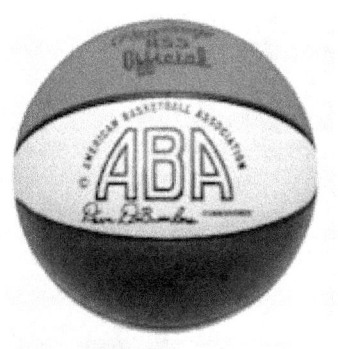

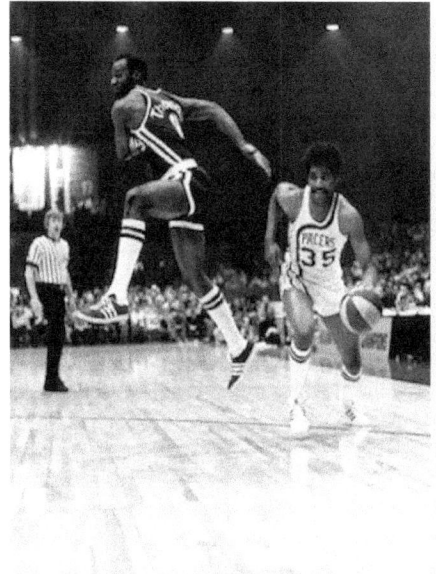

Roger Brown

George McGinnis

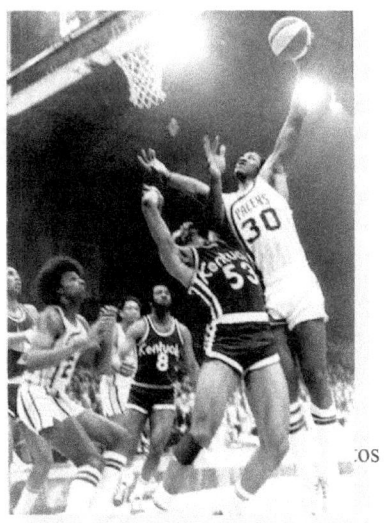

:os

Steve Fox photos
Arthur Hundausen Collection

33

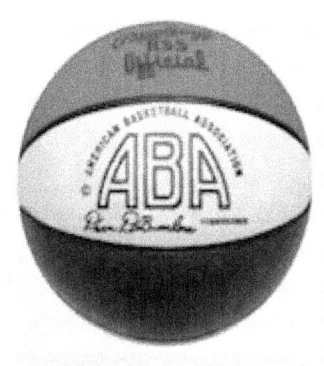

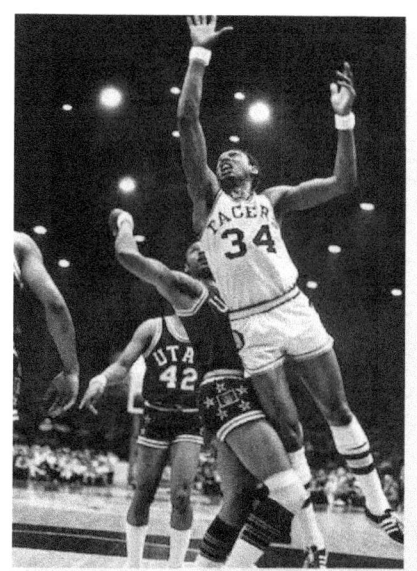

Mel Daniels

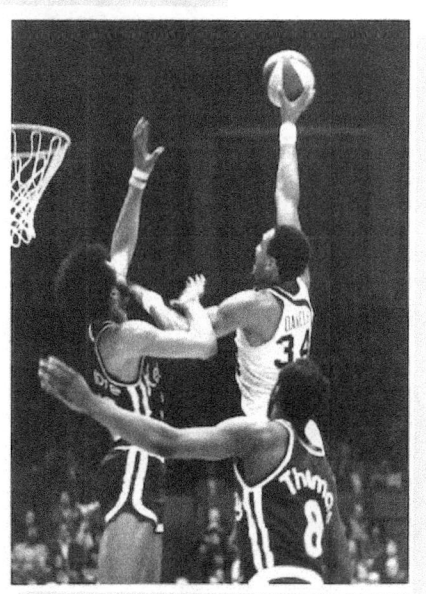

Steve Fox photos
Arthur Hundausen Collection

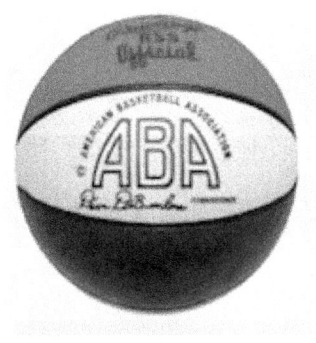

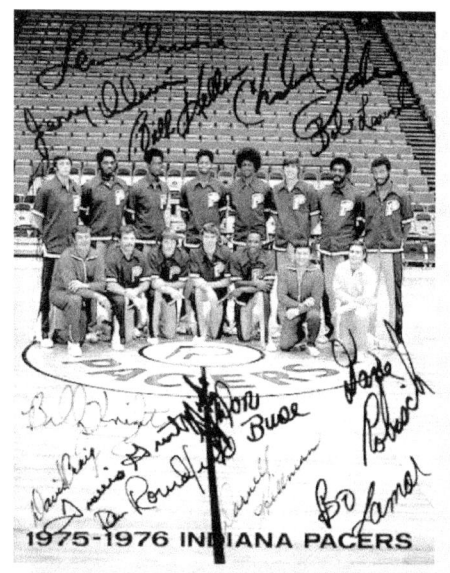

1975-1976 INDIANA PACERS

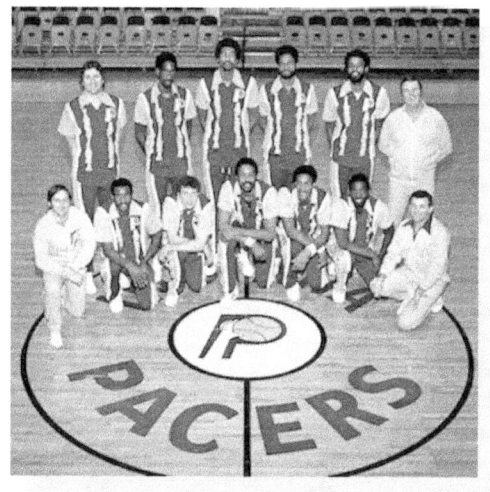

Steve Fox team photos

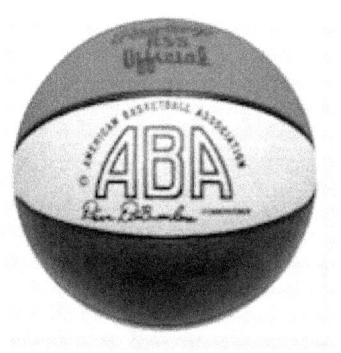

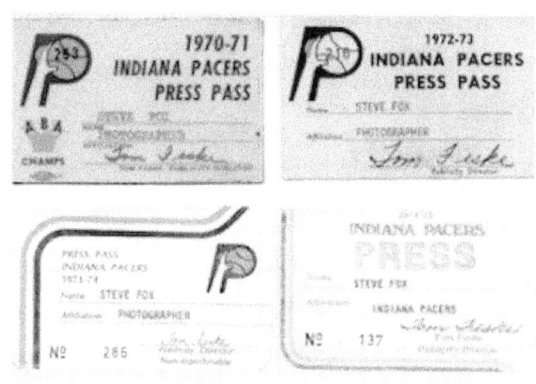

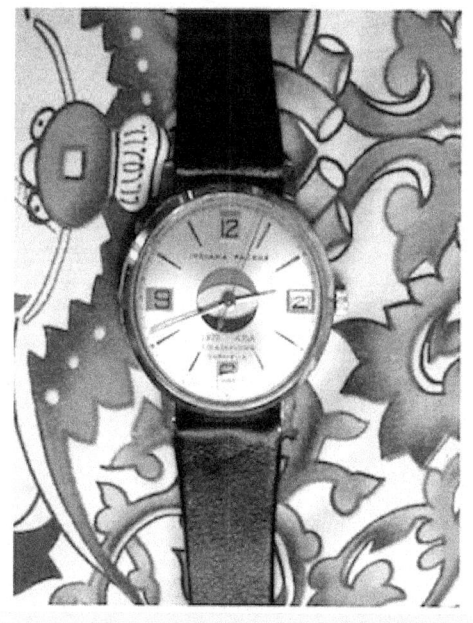

Pacer Collection

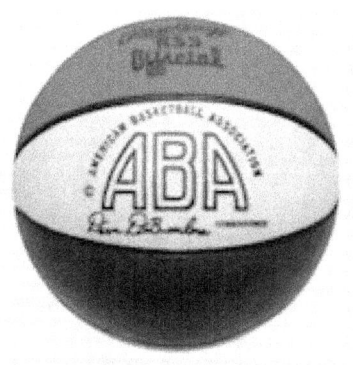

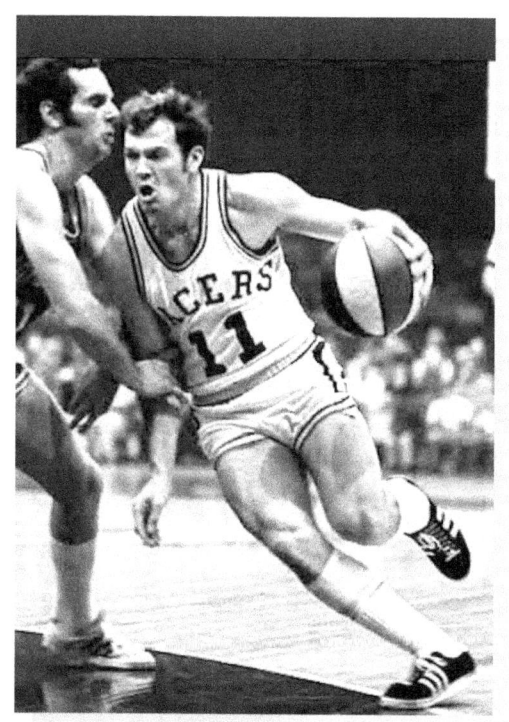

Billy Keller

ABA home offices

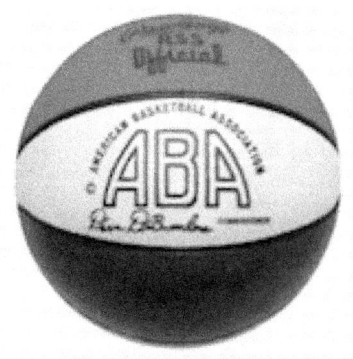

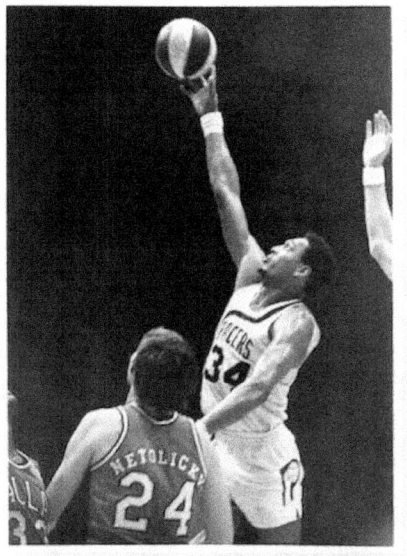 Mel Daniels

Donnie Freeman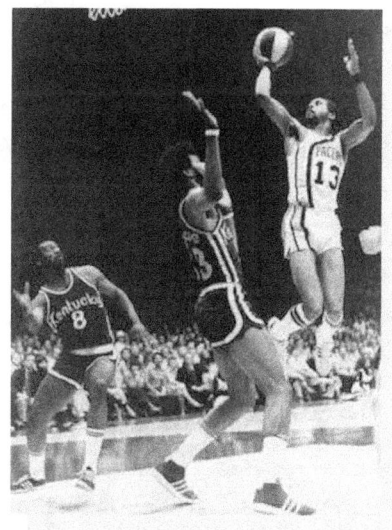

Steve Fox photos
Arthur Hundausen Collection

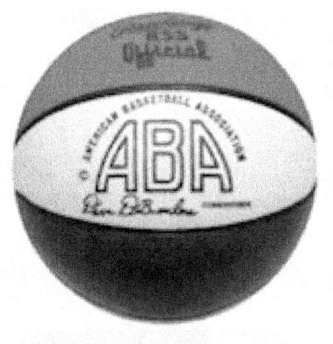

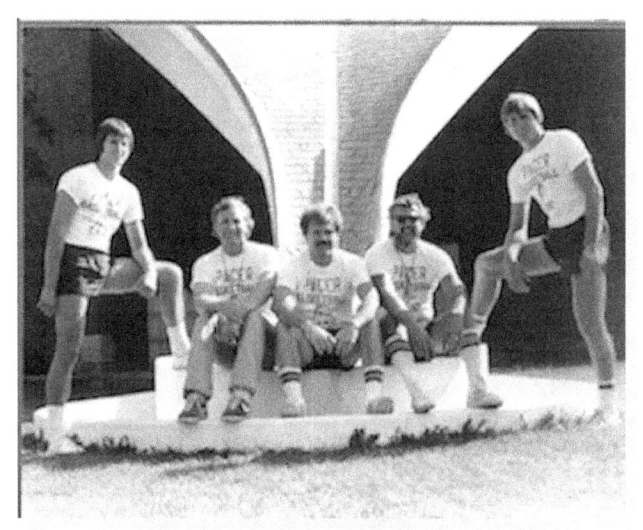

Bill Keller's summer camp, Anderson, Indiana

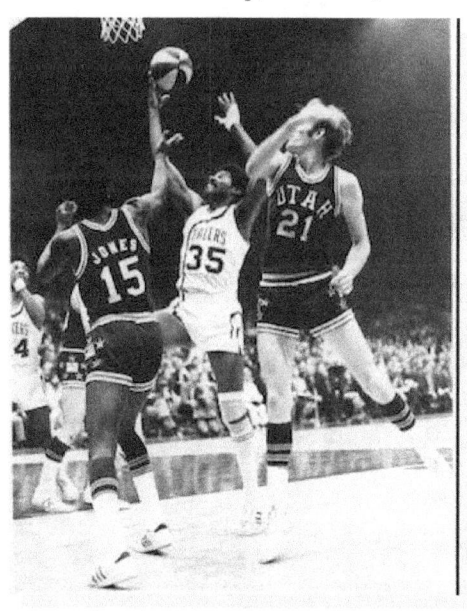

Roger Brown
Steve Fox photos
Arthur Hundausen Collection

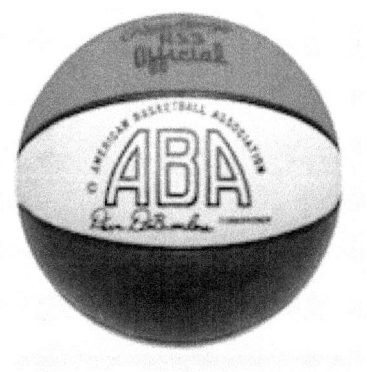

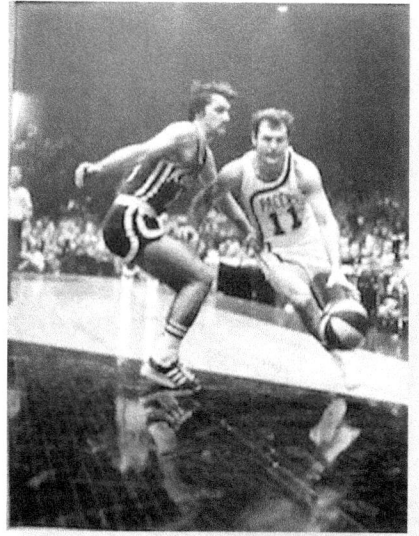

Billy Keller

Johnny Neumann

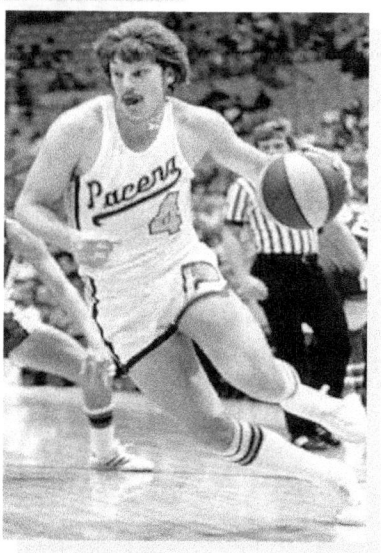

Steve Fox photos
Arthur Hundausen Collection

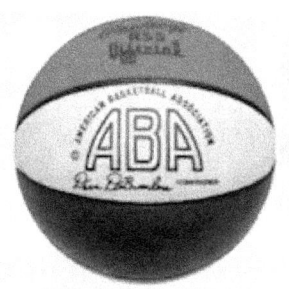

Chapter 3

# Pacers Move to Market Square Arena

# 1974

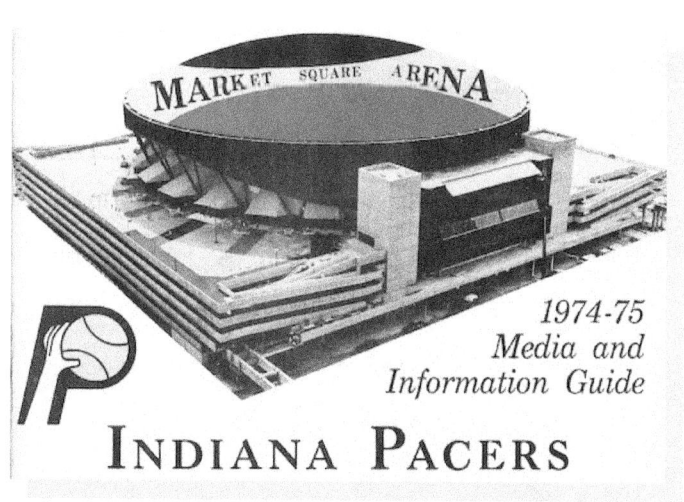

1974-75
*Media and
Information Guide*

INDIANA PACERS

# A New Home

There was a stark difference between the Fairgrounds Coliseum and Market Square Arena. You parked your car inside the building, the halls were brightly lit, the paint was new, and everything had a new smell to it.

The arena had the largest seating capacity of any building I had ever been in. Seeing seating for 18,000 people was breathtaking, and the building was so large it made the playing floor look small.

I had hoped the lighting would be better at Market Square Arena, but as it turned out the lighting was at best about the same as it was at the Fairgrounds Coliseum. The film speed was rated at 1600 ASA, 250th of a second, 5.6 f stop, and unfortunately the pictures had less contrast. I had hoped for better.

Once in Market Square Arena the Pacers would fill the seats in their first year. But in their second year, while still in the ABA, many of the teams encountered money problems and began to drop out of the league, leaving the stronger teams to make more frequent trips to Indianapolis to play the Pacers (with the stars of the remaining teams coming more frequently and me selling more color oils to their players).

As the second-year in Market Square Arena started, the attendance went from a full house to about nine thousand people on average. Seeing all those empty seats in the background of my pictures always made me grimace.

My Dad and I would make frequent trips to Louisville, Kentucky, to photograph the Colonel games, especially when the Pacers and the New York Nets with Julius Erving would play. I could make the trip there and back in a little more than six hours, so I barely had time to make it to work the next day. One thing about the Kentucky Colonels was that they always played before a sellout crowd.

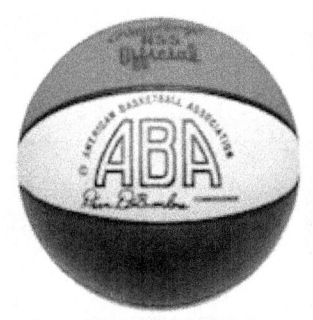

Market Square Arena

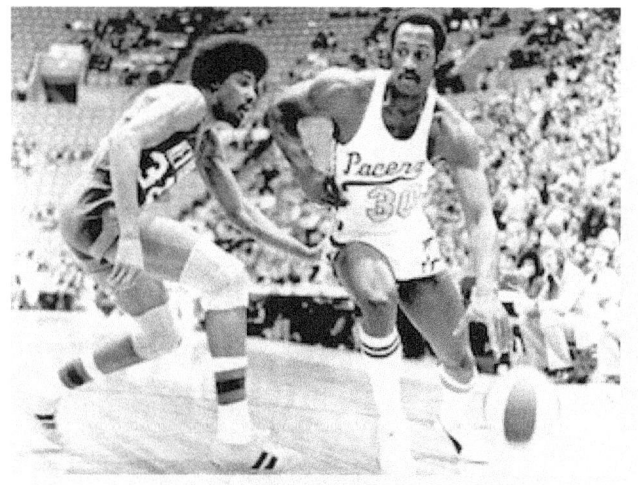

Julius "Dr. J" Erving and George McGinnis

Billy Knight

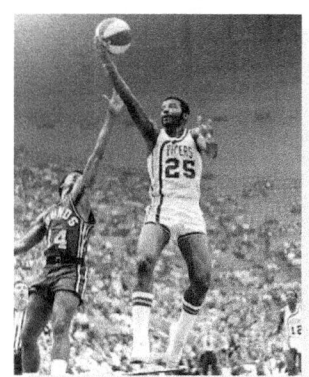

Steve Fox photos

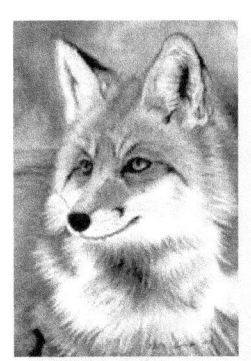

# Chapter 4

# New Beginnings in the

# NBA

## October 21, 1976

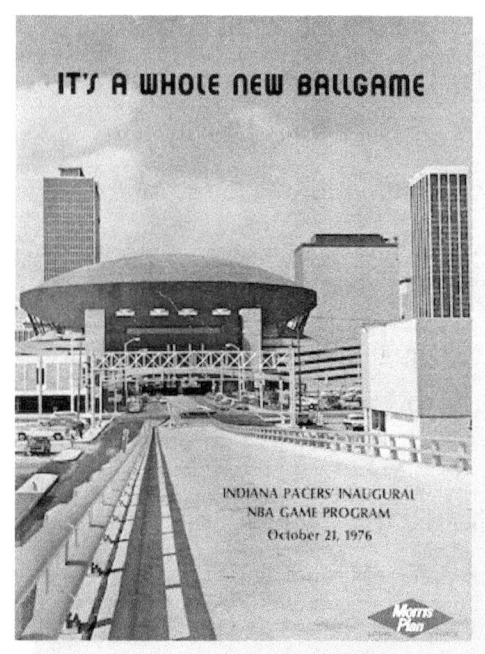

IT'S A WHOLE NEW BALLGAME

INDIANA PACERS' INAUGURAL
NBA GAME PROGRAM
October 21, 1976

# Pacers Make It into the NBA

The Pacers first game in the NBA was October 21, 1976, against the Boston Celtics. The game was a sellout. It was good to get on with basketball without all the money troubles of the past.

The league at that time was made up of all the original NBA teams plus the four ABA teams that joined the NBA, which allowed me to focus on some new players.

It was exciting for me to see all the players that I had watched on television, now in person.

The teams came to Indianapolis once a year, other than those in the Pacers' division. One noticeable difference was the style of play. The NBA was more structured, unlike the ABA, which was wide-open basketball. The other difference between the leagues for me was that brown basketball, which could barely be noticed in the pictures. In the ABA, that red, white, and blue basketball was highly visible.

After the Pacers entered the NBA, the pregame photo assignments greatly increased with honorary ball boys shooting free throws hoping for a free savings account from an Indianapolis bank, local businesses and corporations taking part in pregame promotions, Playboy magazine centerfold girls, Miss Indiana, and visiting dignitaries taking part in group photographs with the players.

This was the first year I did color oils for the program covers, and I would then make a pregame presentation of the original color oil to the player.

Many players I had known over the years were gone soon after the Pacers entered the NBA. Other players that remained were soon to be traded off. It's the part of pro basketball that it is hard to take, but it is part of playing in pro sports.

Another noticeable effect of the move into the NBA was that people who'd had courtside seats in the old venue and whom I'd gotten to know were now dispersed to other seats in the new Market Square Arena.

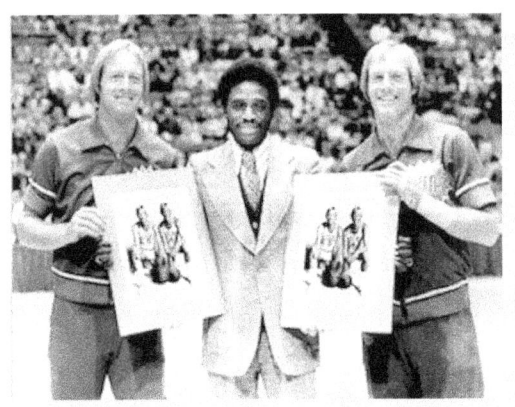

Tom and Dick VanArsdale of the Phoenix Suns

holding color oils

Steve Fox photo

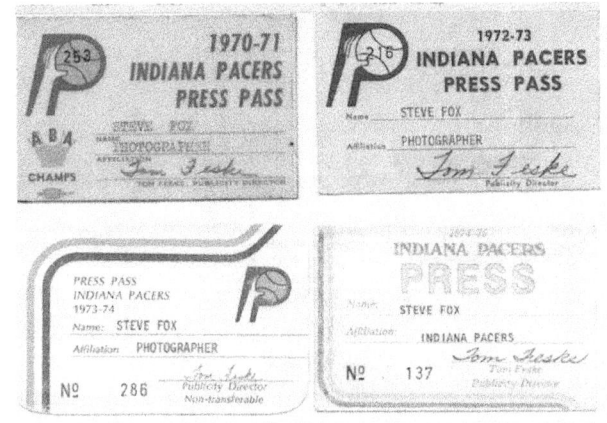

Photographer passes

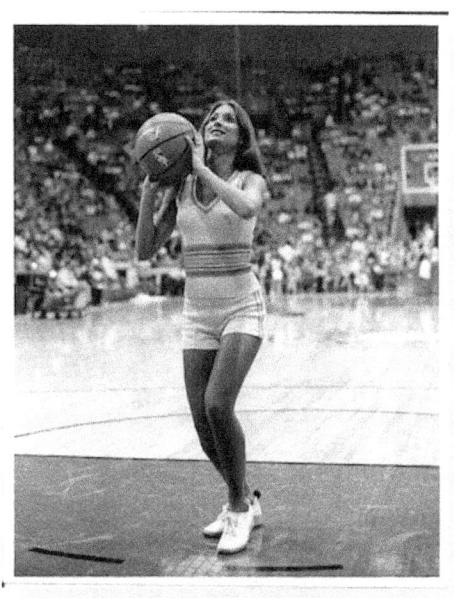

Barbara Mowgin, Miss Indiana First Runner-Up
Steve Fox photos

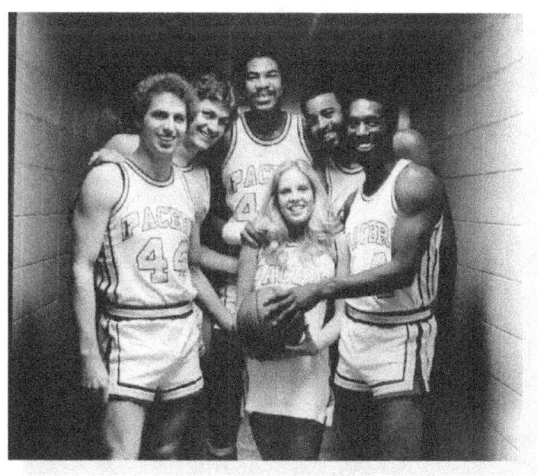

Pamela Bryant of Indianapolis
Miss Playmate Centerfold April 1978

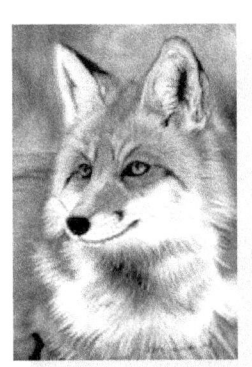

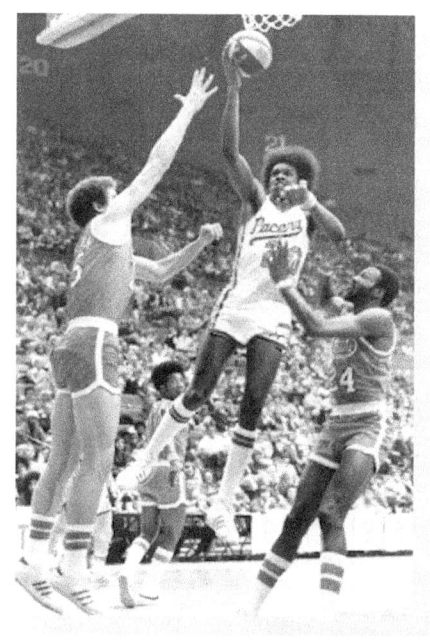

Darnell Hillman

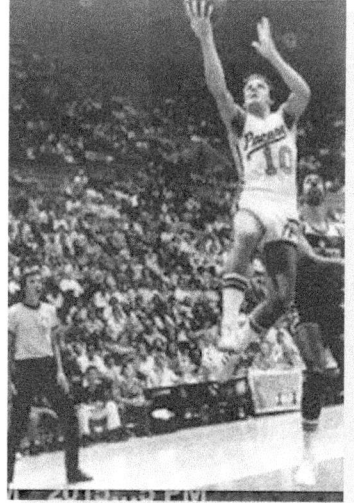

Don Buse

Steve Fox photos
Arthur Hundausen Collection

61

# The Pacemates

The Pacemates had never entertained such a large audience before the NBA. What's more, not only did they entertain for three or more hours during a game, but they also worked during the week at Pacer functions and practice sessions. Many even performed while injured.

Entering the NBA opened up new opportunities for business promotions using the Pacemates and my photographs.

As for my photo assignments, the Pacemates were always there for group photos with the guests, honorary ball boys, and various dignitaries.

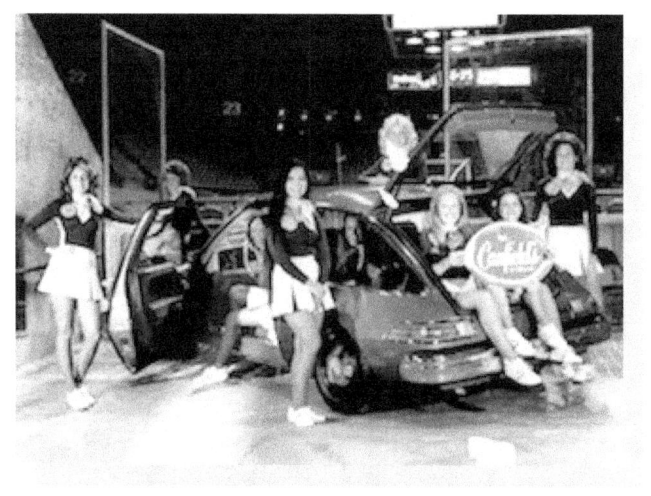

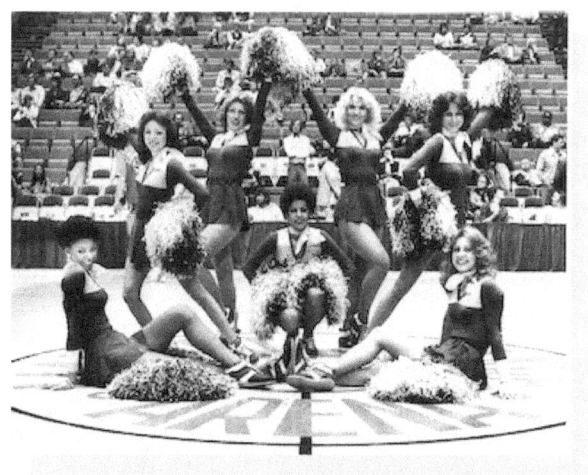

Pacers Pacemates
Steve Fox photos

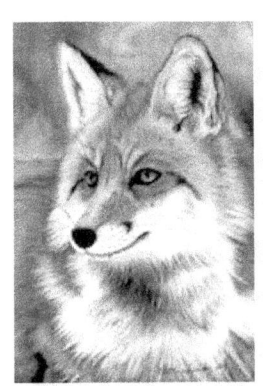

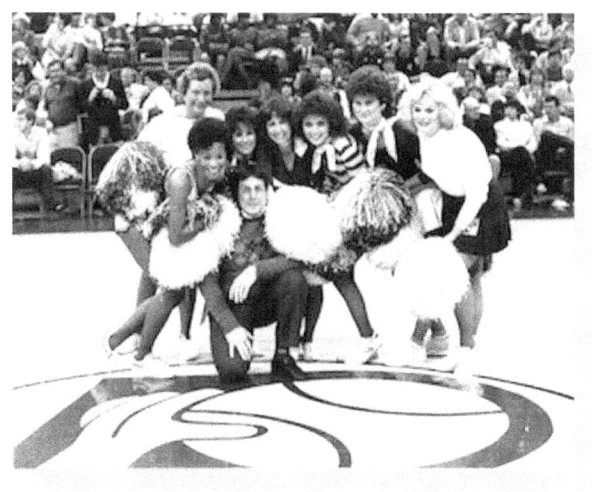

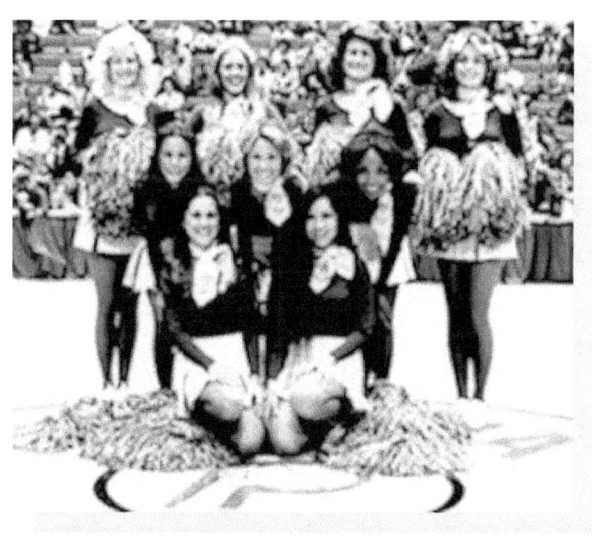

Pacers Pacemates
Steve Fox photos

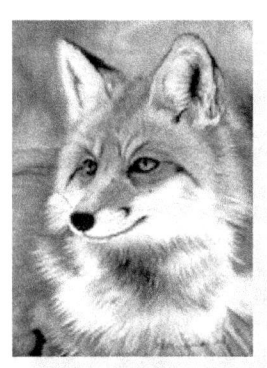

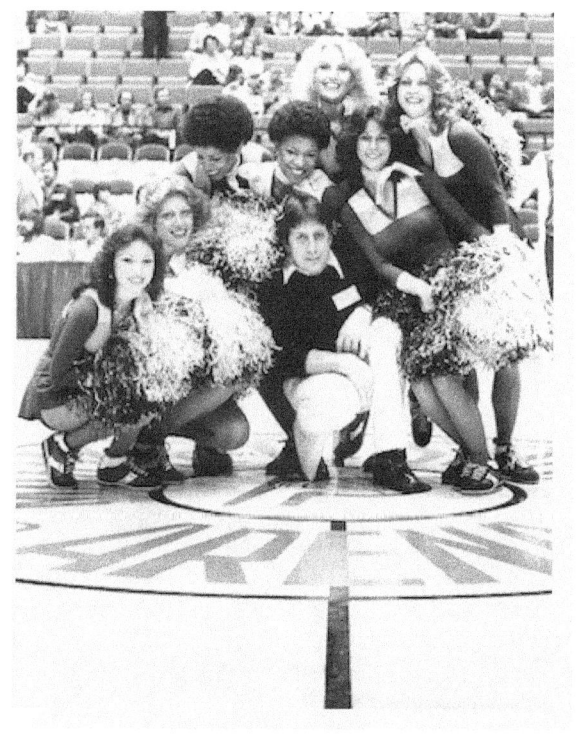

Pacers Pacemates

Martin Fox photo

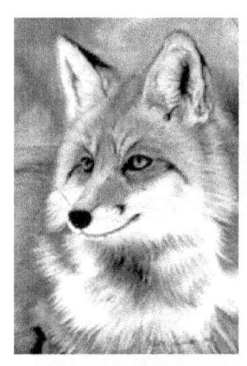

# NBA All-Star Game
# February 13, 1977

This was the first NBA All-Star game since the entry of the four ABA teams: the Indiana Pacers, Denver Nuggets, New York Nets, and San Antonio Spurs.

The NBA All-Star game was being played in Milwaukee, Wisconsin, at the Milwaukee Mecca Arena. My dad and I flew round-trip the same day to the game, as the Pacers had gotten both of us photo credentials.

The arena was filled to capacity, and the lighting was great thanks to the lights the TV network suspended from the ceiling. It was a very good game with the three Pacers players each having a good game as well.

Don Buse and Billy Knight made the All-Star Western team. Darnell Hillman won the Slam-Dunk contest. Don Buse finished the game with four points and two rebounds, and he handed out five assists and made four steals. Billy Knight finished with four points and five rebounds, and he made two steals. Julius Erving received the NBA All-Star Most Valuable Player Award.

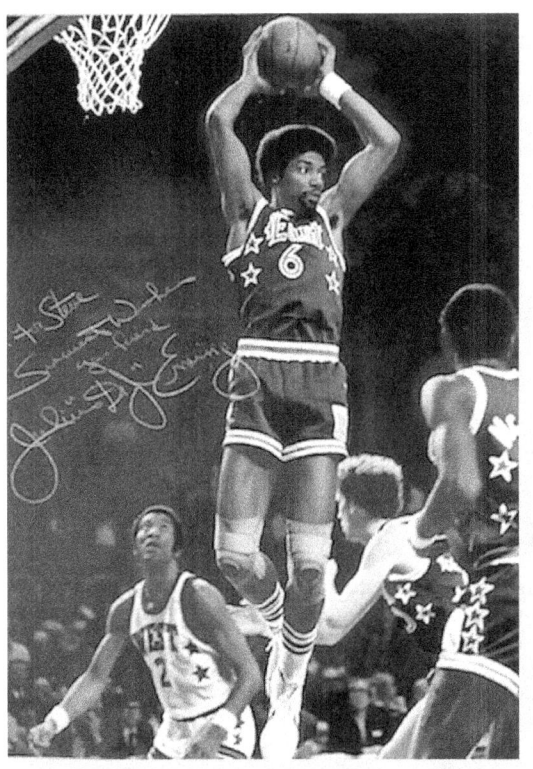

Julius "Dr. J" Erving
Steve Fox photo

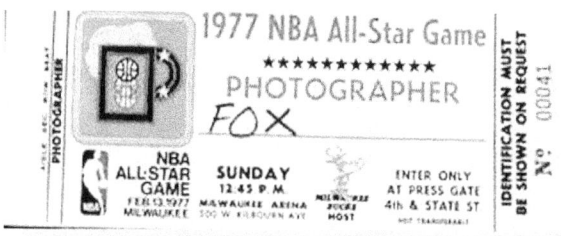

1977 All-Star game pass

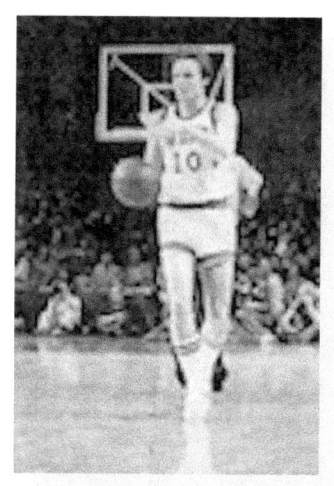

Don Buse
Western All-Stars

Steve Fox photo

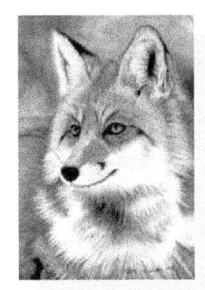

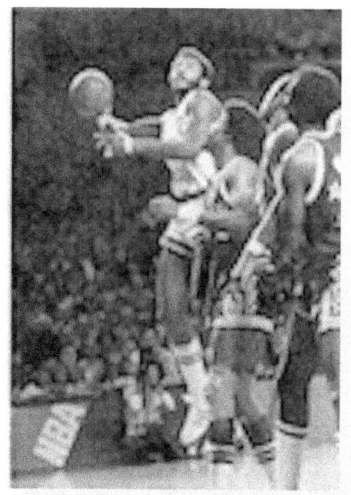

Billy Knight
Western All-Stars

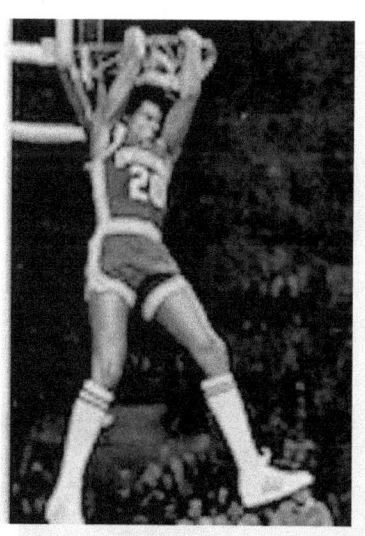

Darnell Hillman won the NBA Slam-Dunk contest

Steve Fox photos

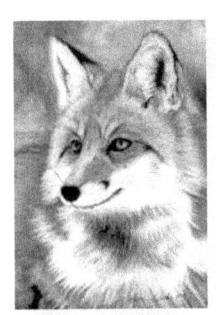

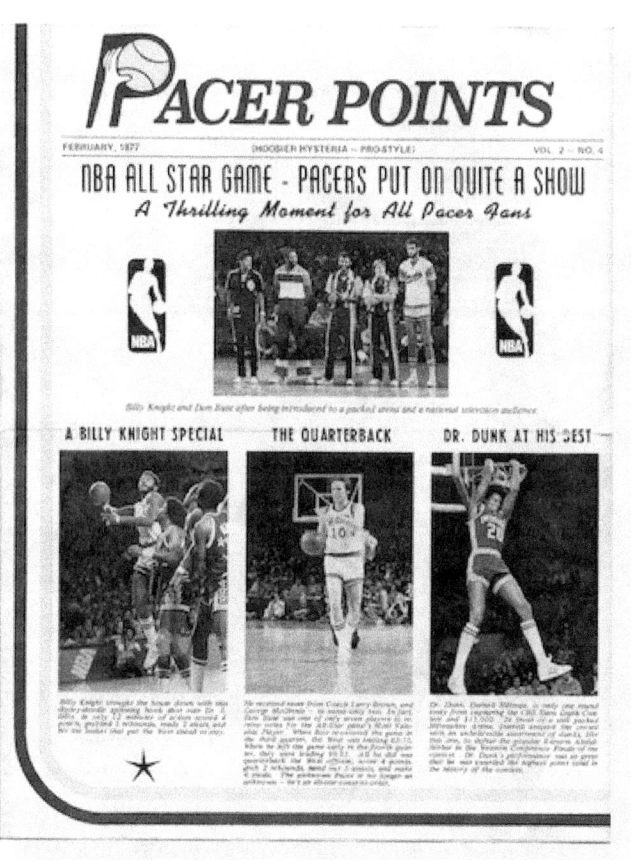

Steve Fox photos

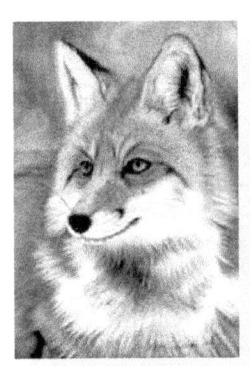

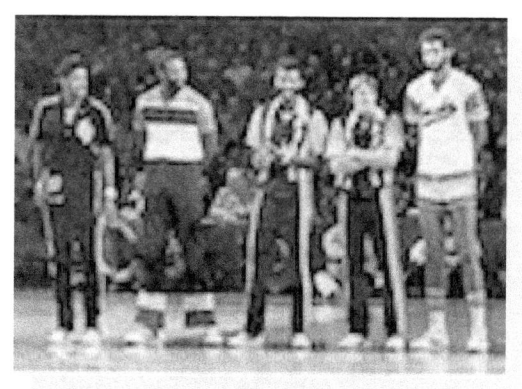

NBA All-Star pregame introductions

Left to right
Maurice Lucas, Bob Lanier, Billy Knight, Don Buse,
Kareem Abdul-Jabbar

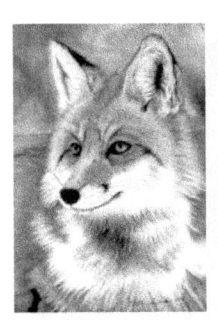

# Julius " Dr. J" Erving

The first time I saw Julius Irving he was with the Virginia Squires in the 1971–72 season. As a sports photographer I could tell he was special even in the pregame warm-ups. I would soon find out that he was not only a great young talent but also a great guy. The Indianapolis fans got to see his talents many times during the year. Because of the rotation of the teams left in the ABA, the Squires would play the Pacers several times a month.

I thoroughly enjoyed my time on the basketball floor taking pictures of Dr. J. I had started branching out doing color oils for Pacers program covers and also selling action color oils to the players. I had a photographer's pass that would allow me access to both the Pacers and visitor dressing rooms. After one of the early season games I got to speak to Dr. J. He was interested in my color oils, and he purchased my first color oil of him. I still remember he was going to give this color oil to his mother. It was an honor for me, as it turned out that this one would be the first of many he would be purchasing over the years.

I was fortunate to have the support of my family in my work as a sports photographer over the years. My love of sports photography grew as a second job, but I was gone a lot of evenings. The advantage of being part of the Pacers family was that my family had the opportunity to get close to the players. I have two sons, and they were fans not only of the Pacers but also (and especially) Dr. J. To this day I still remember how exciting it was for them to have Julius take time out to have his picture taken with them. It definitely gave my boys special status at school the next day.

I always saw Julius as very personable and friendly to all his fans. Even as he grew to superstar status, he always remained the same person.

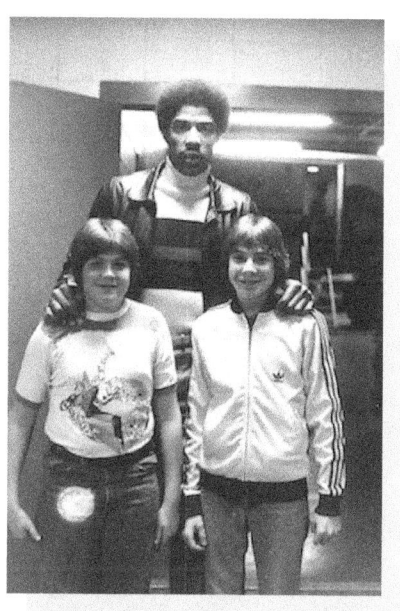

My two sons, Rob and Tim, with Julius Erving

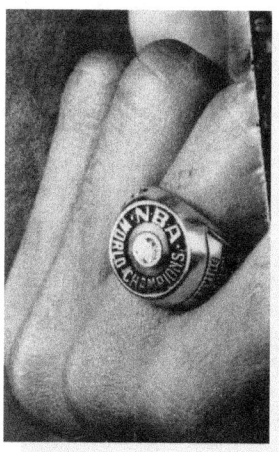

Julius Erving's 1983 NBA World Championship Ring

Steve Fox photos

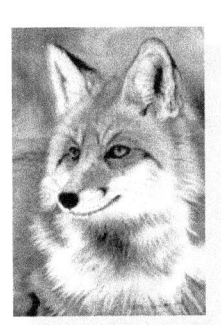

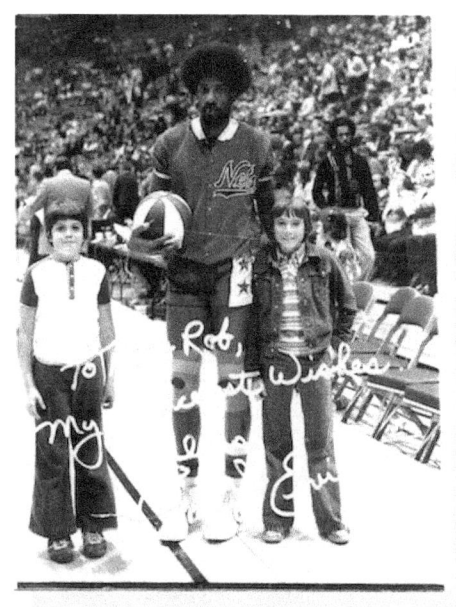

Rob and Tim with Julius Erving

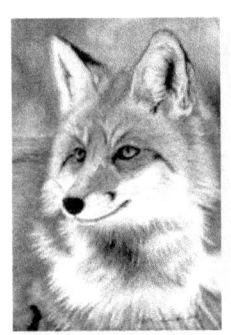

# Chapter 5

# Color Oils in Sports Photography

I had been doing color oils for several years before my introduction to the ABA. I worked mainly with Indy cars and sprint cars, so I was no beginner in the use of cameras and color oils. I had always liked art, so mixing the two forms together seemed natural. As far as composition they are almost the same and pleasing to the eye.

After a couple seasons taking action pictures of the Pacers it started to feel repetitive. My first successful color oil (after several attempts) was of Billy Keller, a guard for the Pacers. It was a challenge trying to capture the perfect black and white negative and develop it to an 11x14-inch print to do a color oil. This challenge would not only benefit me but also the Pacers. This opportunity to do color oils would last many years.

# What Are Color Oils?

Color oils are a translucent color in a tube like one would use in canvas painting. The different colors come in squeeze tubes, and you use a pallet for grouping your colors and mixing for different shading.

You are basically working on a black-and-white paper picture with a canvas-like textured finish. I used Kodak tapestry developing paper, mounted on art board, and I usually worked with 11x14-inch to 16x20-inch pictures.

I would apply the colors with cotton balls, wooden skewers, and cotton swabs. Darker color oils were applied on darker portions of the picture, lighter colors on the light areas. Marshals color kits are still available on the Internet.

The color oils take about twenty-four hours to dry. The advantages of color oils over color prints are that they are hand-done, will never fade out, and each picture is one-of-a-kind. No machine printing is used to make a color oil.

# Market for Color Oils

Athletes and pro sports people were my main market, but I also did color oils of racehorses, homes, collector cars, boats, and racecars.

I never had an off-season doing these pictures; the work I did had year-round appeal. It was basically for people who wanted exclusivity hanging on their walls at home or at their businesses, or who wanted to give them as gifts.

# Getting Into Sports Photography

If you are thinking about getting into pro sports photography, you will not only need to be very good but also very lucky. The sports world is looking for the best photographers, and there are only so many who will be able to sit on that floor. With all the fine cameras in the world nowadays your work will be somewhat easier, but the equipment is very expensive. Even with all that expensive equipment, however, you will be the one taking that picture. You need to have confidence in your ability and be able to justify the cost of getting involved in sports photography.

I had the opportunity to be associated with many franchises and to be compensated for my work, but when I was in pro sports most guys were never involved to the degree I was.

My advice to get started is to get involved in all local sports. Perhaps you could get credentials through your local newspaper. No matter how hard it may be to get into this business, for me it was a dream come true and one I will never forget.

Even if you don't get rich from the experience, being involved from a camera perspective close to the action is like a dream come true for someone who loves sports. I wish everyone could experience the thrill at least once.

These pictures are from my personal collection of color oils and are 11x14 inches, and the bottom one is 16x20 inches and can be found on the back cover.

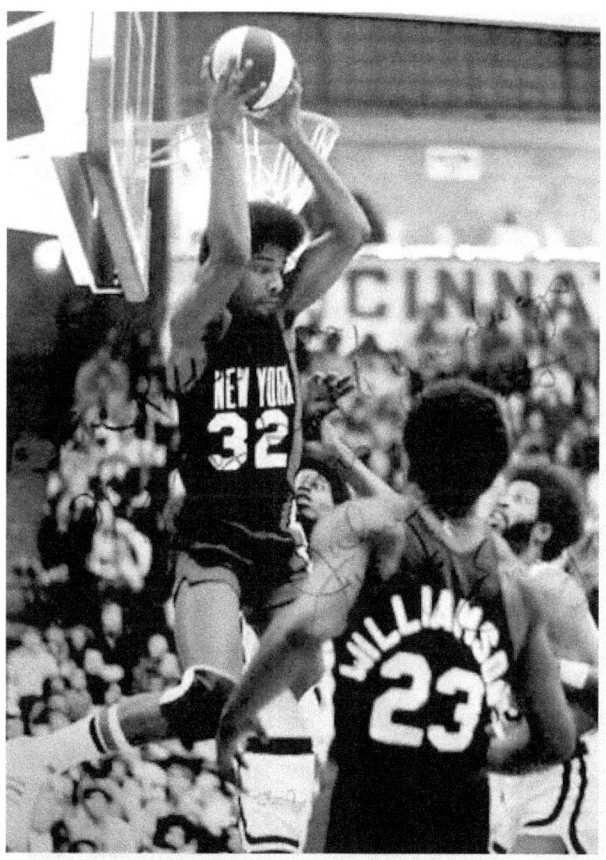

Julius "Dr. J" Erving

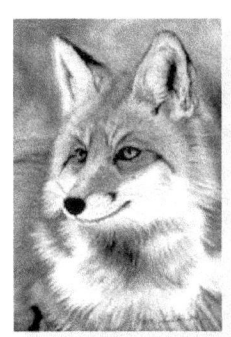

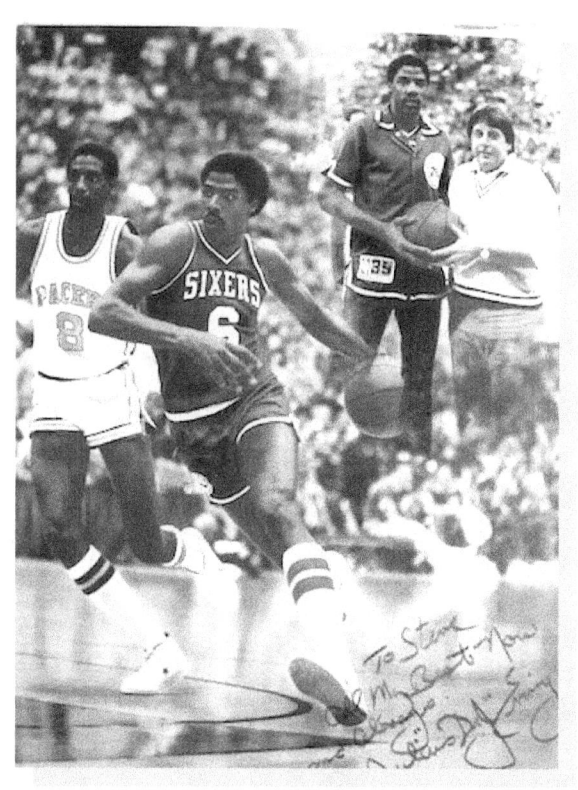

Julius "Dr J" Erving and myself

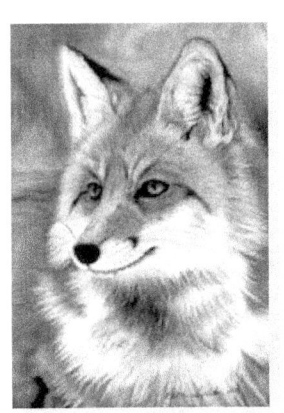

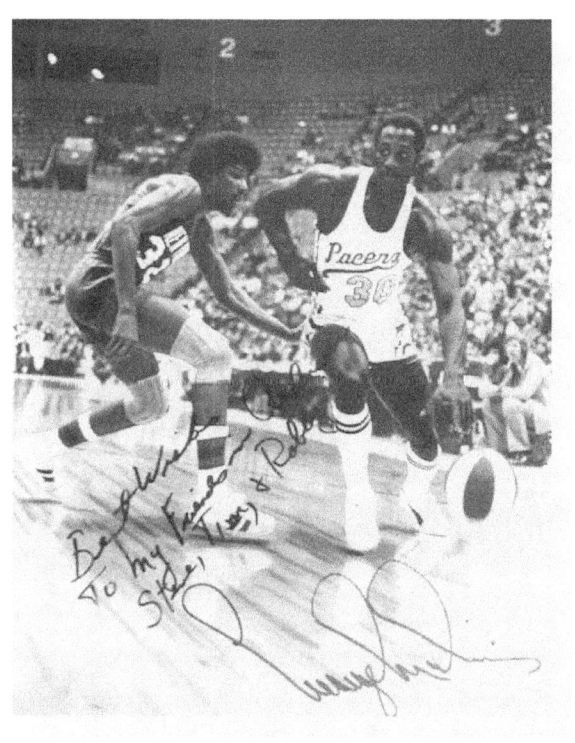

Julius "Dr. J" Erving and George McGinnis

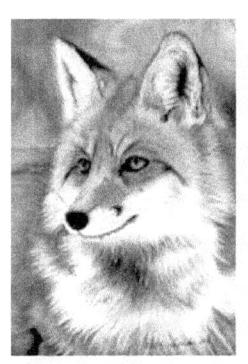

Some of the other pictures I've taken over the years and made color oils out of them.

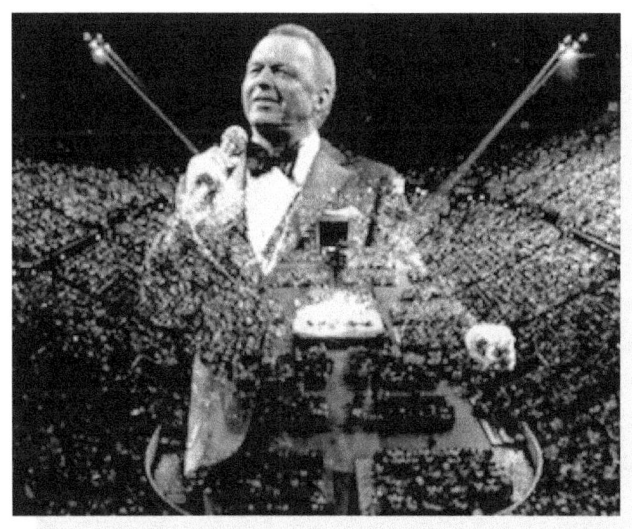

Frank Sinatra in the round at Market Square Arena

May 1976

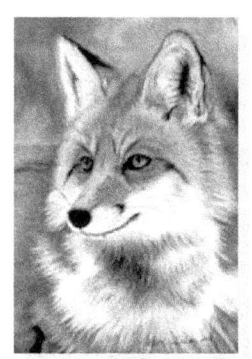

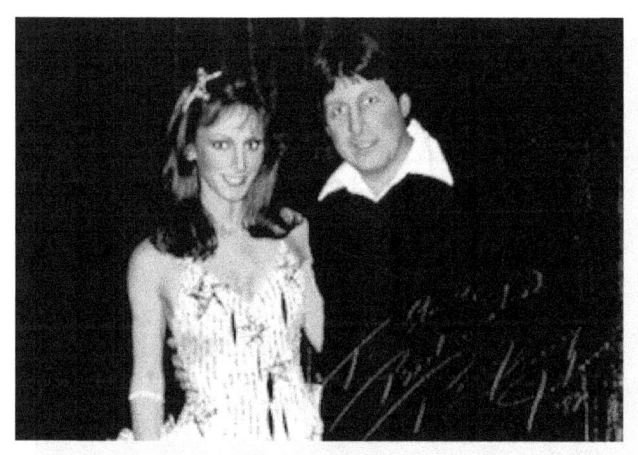

Peggy Fleming 1968 Olympic Champion

Three-time World Champion

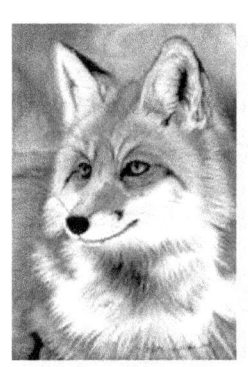

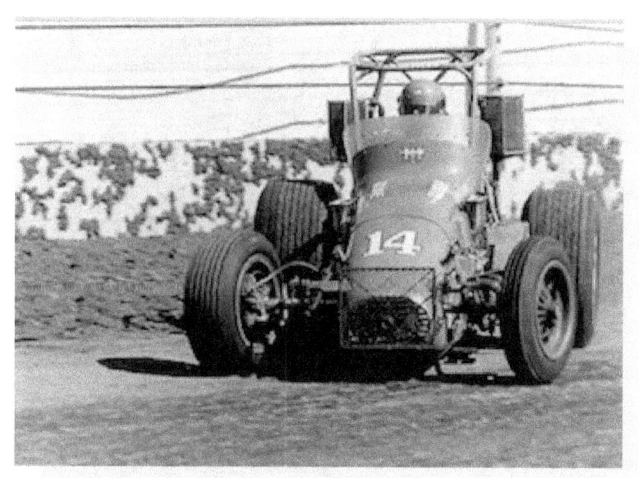

AJ Foyt at the Hoosier Hundred

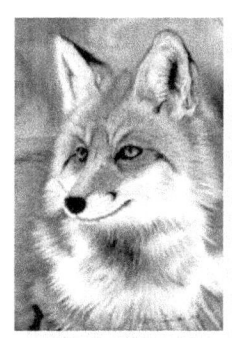

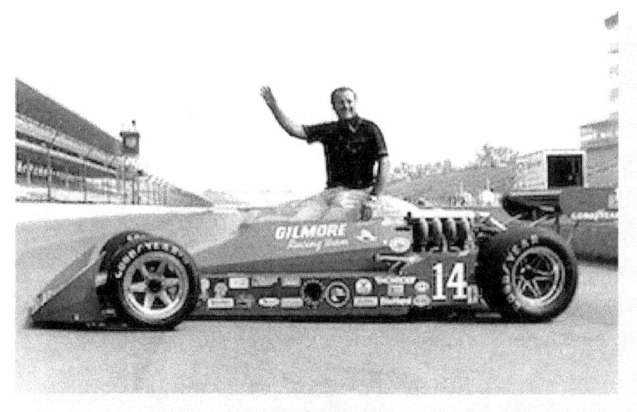

AJ Foyt, Four-Time Indianapolis 5oo Winner

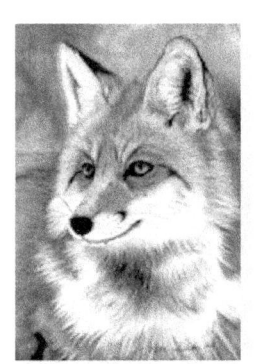

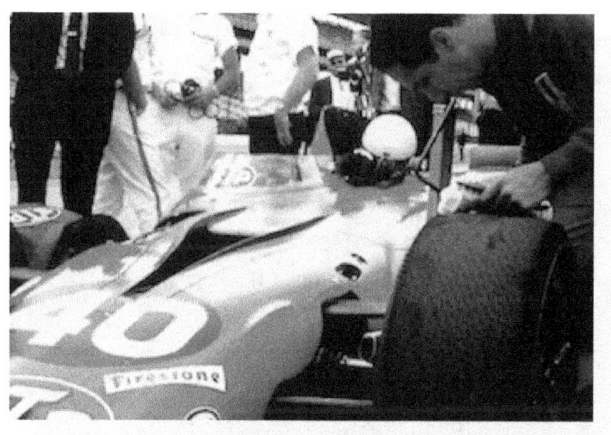

STP Turbine car driven by Parnelli Jones at the Indianapolis 500 in 1967, owner Andy Granatelli

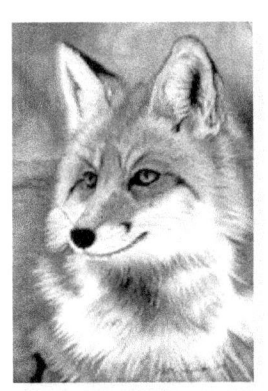

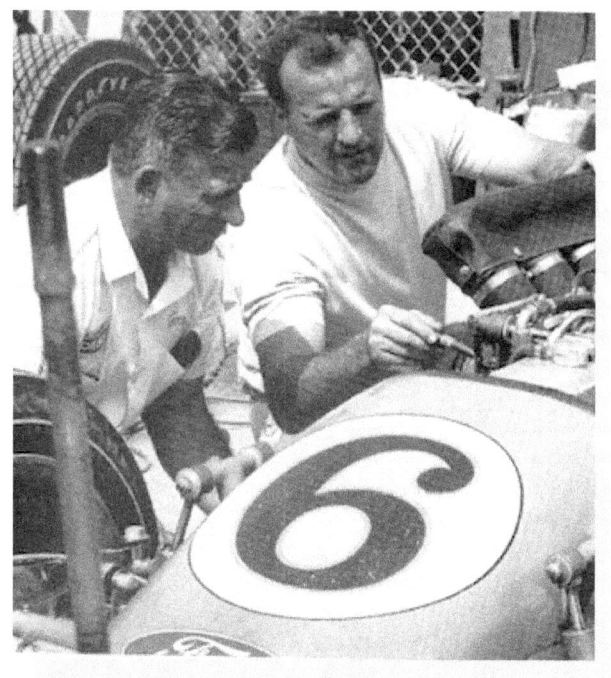

AJ Foyt and his dad, Tony Foyt, at the Indianapolis State
Fairgrounds Hoosier Hundred

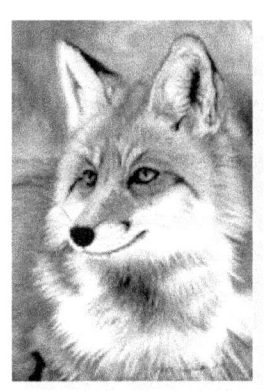

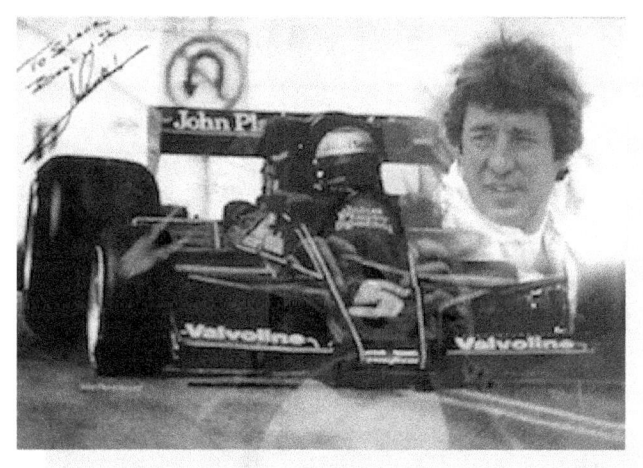

Mario Andretti, 1978 Formula One Champion

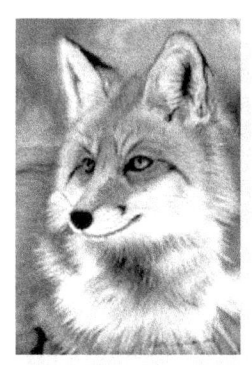

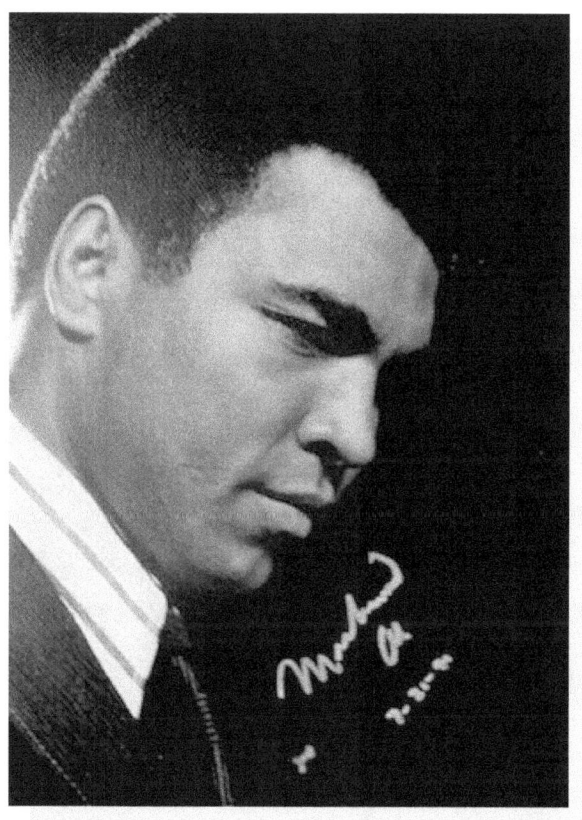

I took this picture of Ali during Homecoming Night at Freedom Hall in Louisville, Kentucky, a month after he defeated George Foreman in Zaire, Africa, 1978 for the Heavyweight Championship of the World.

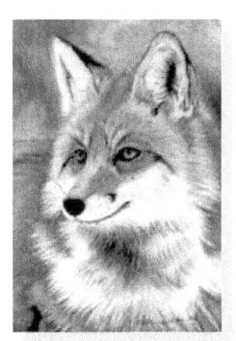

# Chapter 6

# Bobby and Nancy Leonard

Even though I've lost contact with the Leonards since I left the Pacers, I haven't forgotten them. Without Bobby I would never have had an opportunity to be with the Pacers. Through that opportunity I have an abundance of happy memories from that special period in my life that I can share with other Pacers fans.

Bobby and Nancy's tireless work over the years, along with many other people, helped build the Pacers franchise and gave Indiana status in the world of sports. They were the forerunners who helped Indianapolis grow as a sports city.

I watched the PBS special that was shown about Bobby's life. It provided a glimpse of his early life in Terre Haute, Indiana, where he was raised. Born in the industrial part of town, his personality was formed there and helped make him the great man he became.

Nancy always worked just as hard as Bobby in the early years of the Pacers, overseeing the details of the Pacers office as well as taking care of their family. If you were a fan of the Pacers in the early years, you will remember seeing her as a loyal fan waving her gold scarf in the front row.

One of things I remember most from the PBS special on Bobby Leonard was this bit of advice from Bobby: "Your friends are your extended family. Always love them as though they were your family." This sums up the feeling I have about the Leonard family.

# Chapter 7

# My Family

I worked at General Motors for thirty-nine years as an hourly worker. My hours were 5:00 am. to 1:30 pm. I found working in a factory day in and day out to be tedious and not much of a challenge, so when the opportunity came to join the Pacers as a photographer I went for it. I had always liked art and photography. Doing the Pacers photography work in the darkroom was very time-consuming, and by the mid-seventies I had begun taking Market Square Arena publicity pictures when they had entertainers come in.

I was traveling to Indianapolis three to four times a week plus spending many hours in the darkroom doing developing and working on color oils at the same time. The trip to the Fairgrounds Coliseum in Indianapolis from Anderson was about eighty miles round-trip. When the Pacers moved to Market Square Arena downtown the round-trip distance increased to about 100 miles. As you can see, I was gone a lot of the time.

I had a wife and two sons at home, but thankfully my lovely wife understood that I needed a challenge in life outside the factory. I am very grateful for working at General Motors and for my union, the UAW. My family would never have had the life we enjoyed if not for GM and the UAW.

So, in conclusion, this chapter is really about my wife, Deanna. If not for her support my photography in the ABA and NBA would have been impossible. She would tend to the boys at home while I was gone, so when I was home it was precious time together. I'm eternally grateful to my wife for allowing me to fulfill a dream.

# Chapter 8

# My Father and Me

When I started this book about the American Basketball Association and Indiana Pacers I didn't realize the direction I would eventually take.

I started out with the goal to share some of my experiences and my photography, but I realized it was more about a father and son finally finding a common interest after a rocky relationship through my early years and life. He tried to understand where we were different and find a common interest to no avail. He was a stamp collector, and I collected turtles. He and my mother loved ballroom dancing, and I liked rivers and mud. He had long, black, wavy hair, and people called him "Inky" because of his hair. I had brown hair and a flat top, I liked to work with my hands and get dirty; he wore white shirts and ties. Even after he got home from work he still wore white shirts. I even remember him mowing the lawn in white shirts when I was young.

Soon after I started taking photos for the Pacers in 1969 I got my Dad a photographer's pass. That was the beginning of our father-son relationship—I was thirty years old. We traveled back and forth to the games and took road trips together with the Pacers. We had finally found a common denominator in our lives, and for the next fifteen years we grew to be not only father and son but also the best of friends for life.

I miss my Dad. I miss the ABA.

I miss………………………………….

www.ingramcontent.com/pod-product-compliance
Lightning Source LLC
Chambersburg PA
CBHW070811180526
45168CB00002B/574